Contents

One habitat throughout the year   2

In a garden   4

In a pond   6

In the soil and under the leaves   8

On a rocky shore   10

What's for dinner?   12

A place to live   14

At home in an oak tree   16

Down the drain   18

On the rubbish tip   20

A recycling journey   22

Glossary   24

Index   25

One habitat throughout the year

These pictures show the same scene in Spring, Summer, Autumn and Winter.

But are they the same? How many differences between the seasons can you spot?

3

In a garden

Cats are large garden hunters. They catch mice, birds and frogs.

Daisies grow well on lawns. They survive being mown or trampled on.

Aphids live on plants and suck their sap for food.

Hedgehogs hunt in the early mornings or evenings for worms, slugs and insects.

Groundsel is a common weed. It can be found in flower in southern England at any time of year.

Butterflies are attracted by plants such as Buddleias and stinging nettles.

Foxes often come into gardens, even in towns. They feed on small birds and animals or food which they steal from dustbins.

Thrushes break snail shells by bashing them on a stone or path.

Spiders spin large sticky webs. Insects get stuck in the webs and the spiders eat them.

Snails move about when it is damp. You can see the slimy trails they leave behind them. If it is very dry or cold they can seal themselves inside their shells. Snails feed on plants.

Which of the animals in the picture eat other animals and which eat plants?

In a pond

Common reeds grow in the muddy water at the edges of ponds. They have tough bendy stems which can stand up to strong winds without breaking.

Water boatmen swim mainly on their backs and can also fly. They eat tadpoles, insects and small fish.

Dragonfly nymph: the 'nymph' or **larva** of a dragonfly is a ferocious hunter. It has large sucking jaws and catches small fish, tadpoles and other animals.

Tadpoles take about twelve weeks to turn into frogs. They then leave the water and live in damp places on land.

Water mites are related to spiders. They feed on tiny pond animals by piercing them and sucking out their juices.

Take care near water

Duckweed is a floating plant which forms a green carpet on the surface of ponds. Its roots dangle in the water. It provides food for ducks.

Pond snails feed on plants using their tongues and teeth.

Pond skaters use their long middle legs for skating quickly over the pond surface. Their two short front legs are used for picking up dead insects lying on the water.

Ponds are fragile **habitats** which can easily be destroyed. They can dry out or become filled with mud or dead leaves. Rubbish or poisonous chemicals dumped in them can kill off all the wildlife. What can be done to help?

Leeches have a sucker at both ends. They attach themselves to their **prey** and suck out their blood.

In the soil and under the leaves

Some animals are not easy to see at first glance. But if you dig in your garden or look under loose stones or piles of dead leaves you can find many small creatures.

Toads have a dry, warty skin. They do not hop but waddle. They live under piles of leaves or sticks and eat insects which they catch with their long, sticky tongue.

Millipedes have two pairs of legs on each segment. They live in damp soil and eat old leaves and rotten wood.

Earwigs hide away inside flowers, or in dark places. They feed on fallen fruit or flower petals. They use their pincers for fighting.

Earthworms tunnel through the soil. They eat the remains of dead plants and animals in the soil.

Wow! A female woodlouse lays about 200 eggs in a pouch under her body. When they hatch, the babies are carried in the pouch until they can look after themselves.

Woodlice live under stones or dead leaves and feed on dead plants. Some roll up into a ball when frightened.

Slugs live in damp places, such as under stones. They have a long tongue covered with hundreds of teeth which they use to chew plants.

Centipedes live in dark, damp places. They come out after dark to eat insects and slugs. They have one pair of legs on each segment of their body.

What colour are most of these animals?
What shapes are they?
What happens if where they live dries out?

Beetles have a hard covering to their wings.

Ants live in large groups. They tunnel into the soil and make a large nest where the queen ant lays her eggs. They eat insects, seeds and honey.

On a rocky shore

When the **tide** goes out some of the
water is left behind in rock pools. They
may look empty at first, but in fact they
are full of plants and animals.

Periwinkles cling to the
rocks when the tide goes
out. They are protected
from drying out by their
shells. They feed on plants.

Shrimps found in rock pools are
usually transparent and hard to
see until they dart about.

Barnacles attach themselves
to rocks. They poke feathery
arms through the top of their
shell and eat tiny creatures
from the water.

Starfish feed on other small
sea creatures. If they lose
one of their arms, they
quickly grow another one.

Sea anemones look like plants
but are really animals. They
catch their prey with stinging
tentacles.

Crabs hide under overhanging rocks but scuttle out to feed on smaller animals. They are protected by their hard shell.

Bladderwrack is a plant which has hollow pouches to help it float up to the light.

Fish are often difficult to see as they are well **camouflaged** and can slide away into small cracks in the rocks. Most feed on small animals.

Limpets cling so tightly to the rocks that they are very hard to remove. They feed on plants.

What happens to the plants and animals when the tide goes out? How do you think they stand up to being tossed about by the waves breaking against the rocks when the tide comes in?

11

What's for dinner?

A food chain describes what the animals that live in a particular place eat.

In this field, one food chain might be that a rabbit eats grass and a fox eats the rabbit. Can you think of any others?

Here are two more food chains.

pondweed   tadpoles   trout

algae   water fleas   dragonfly larva

What do all the food chains start with?
What would happen if all the plants died?

This is a kind of food chain! What is missing
from this food chain that is in all the others?

There was an old lady who swallowed a fly
I don't know why she swallowed a fly.
Perhaps she'll die.

There was an old lady who swallowed a spider,
That wriggled and wriggled and jiggled inside her.
She swallowed the spider to catch the fly.
I don't know why she swallowed a fly
Perhaps she'll die.

There was an old lady who swallowed a bird.
How absurd, to swallow a bird!
She swallowed the bird to catch the spider. [etc.]

There was an old lady who swallowed a cat.
Well fancy that, she swallowed a cat!
She swallowed the cat to catch the bird. [etc.]

There was an old lady who swallowed a dog.
What a hog, to swallow a dog!
She swallowed the dog to catch the cat. [etc.]

There was an old lady who swallowed a cow.
I don't know how she swallowed the cow!
She swallowed the cow to catch the dog.
She swallowed the dog to catch the cat
She swallowed the cat to catch the bird.
She swallowed the bird to catch the spider,
That wriggled and wriggled and jiggled inside her.
She swallowed the spider to catch the fly.
I don't know why she swallowed a fly.
Perhaps she'll die.

There was an old lady who swallowed a horse.
She's dead of course.

Anon

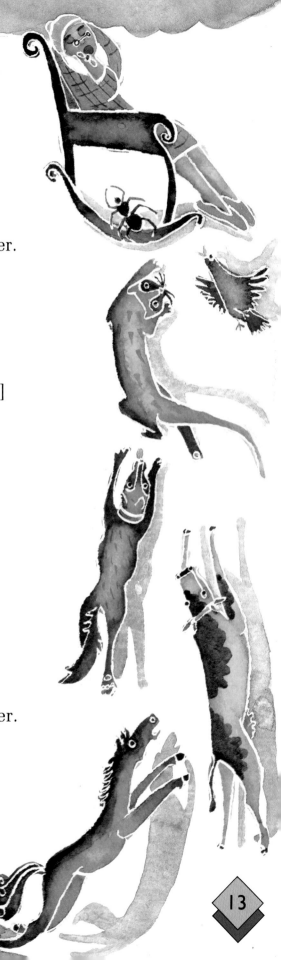

A place to live

Which of these plants and animals do you think could live here? How many of each will you choose? Where will you put them?

Is there anything that might only live there for one season of the year?

You will also need to think of what the animals will eat.

Plants and fungi

an oak tree

mushrooms

poppies

marsh marigolds

rushes

a douglas fir

a beech tree

nettles

clover

dandelions

daisies

a willow

bramble

What might eat them? If you choose too many **predators** you may end up with only one creature left!

What happens to both plants and animals when they die?

Large animals

fish

pied wagtail

tawny owl

fox

pheasant

rabbit

mouse

nuthatch

children

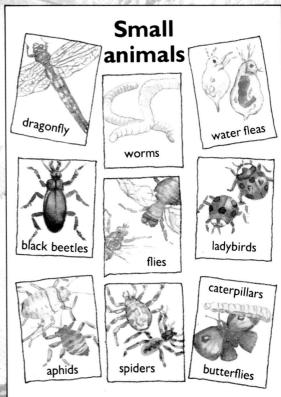

Small animals

dragonfly

worms

water fleas

black beetles

flies

ladybirds

aphids

spiders

caterpillars

butterflies

At home in an oak tree

Oak trees are easy to recognize by their wavy leaves and their nuts called acorns.

Oak wood is hard and lasts well. It has been used for hundreds of years for building houses and boats, furniture, railway wagons, coffins and barrels.

An oak can be home to thousands of birds, plants, fungi and animals. You can see just a few of these in the picture.

Aphids feed on sap from the leaves. The female gives birth several times a day!

Weevils have a long snout that can bore into acorns. They lay their eggs in the hole.

Tree-creepers run up and down the trunk searching for insects which they prise out of the bark with their curved beaks.

Wow!

You can find 284 kinds of insects on one oak tree.

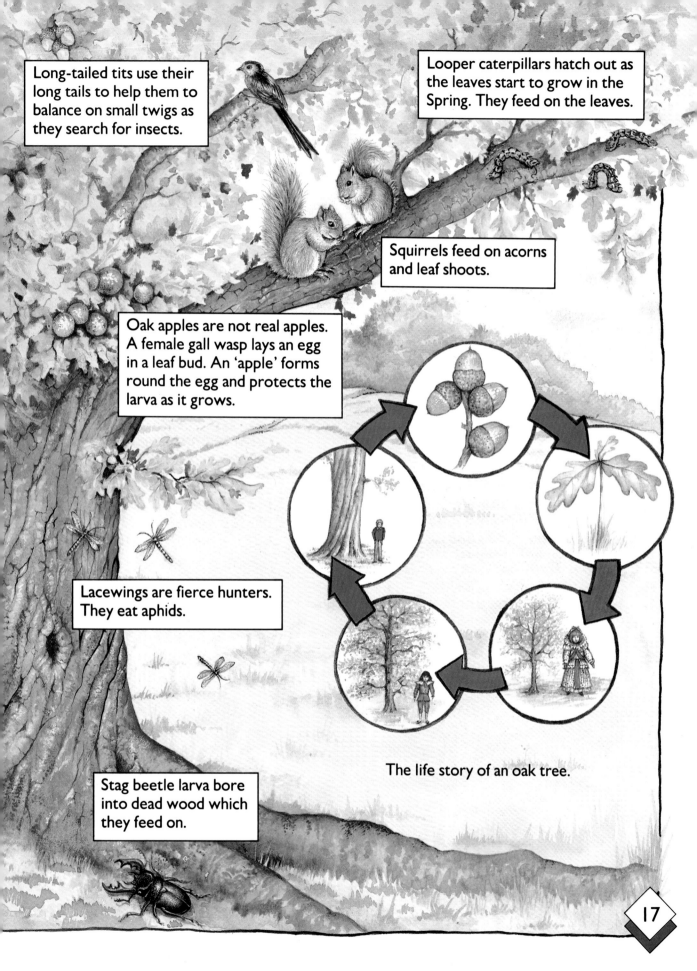

Long-tailed tits use their long tails to help them to balance on small twigs as they search for insects.

Looper caterpillars hatch out as the leaves start to grow in the Spring. They feed on the leaves.

Squirrels feed on acorns and leaf shoots.

Oak apples are not real apples. A female gall wasp lays an egg in a leaf bud. An 'apple' forms round the egg and protects the larva as it grows.

Lacewings are fierce hunters. They eat aphids.

Stag beetle larva bore into dead wood which they feed on.

The life story of an oak tree.

Down the drain

What went down the Flushers' drain? Can you think of
any other things that might end up down your drain?

This is what may happen if the water is too polluted.

On the rubbish tip

Have you read a book called Stig of the Dump? Stig's home was full of things that people didn't want and had thrown away. Here is a description of some of them.

Barney had never seen anything like the collection of bits and pieces, odds and ends, bric-à-brac and old brock, that this Stig creature had lying about his den. There were stones and bones, fossils and bottles, skins and tins, stacks of sticks and hanks of string. There were motor-car tyres and hats from old scarecrows, nuts and bolts and bobbles from brass bedsteads. There was a coal scuttle full of dead electric light bulbs and a basin with rusty screws and nails in it. There was a pile of bracken and newspapers that looked as if it were used for a bed. The place looked as if it had never been given a tidy-up.

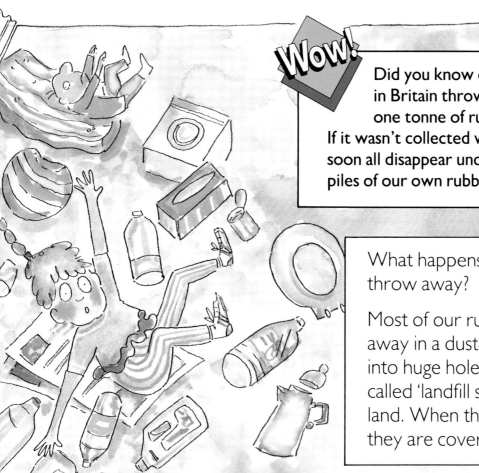

Wow!

Did you know each household in Britain throws away about one tonne of rubbish a year? If it wasn't collected we would soon all disappear under huge piles of our own rubbish!

What happens to things you throw away?

Most of our rubbish is taken away in a dustcart and tipped into huge holes in the ground called 'landfill sites' on waste land. When the holes are full they are covered with soil.

A tip provides ready-made meals for a variety of animals and plants, as you can see from this picture.

Rubbish tips are dangerous places. There may be broken glass or rusty metal. Poisonous chemicals may have been thrown away. Other chemicals and poisonous gases are given off as the waste rots. Some of these gases can also catch fire easily.

Is tipping the best way to get rid of rubbish? Does the waste ever really disappear?

A recycling journey

Milk bottles can be cleaned and re-used if you give them back to the milkman.

If you have a garden you can make a compost heap from your fruit and vegetable peelings. Compost helps plants to grow.

Wow!

Paper is made from trees. Every person in Britain uses six trees' worth of paper every year! So save some trees and use recycled paper.

Don't throw your old clothes away – take them to a charity shop. What you've grown out of or no longer like may be just what someone else is looking for.

Most high streets have bottle banks. You have to separate brown, green, and clear glass.

You can also find places to take your own paper and metal cans. Metal cans should be sorted into steel and aluminium cans (aluminium does not stick to a magnet).

What recycled things do you use? Think of the things you use at school in art and technology.

Glossary

Camouflage
The way in which an animal's colouring or shape blends with its surroundings, helping to hide it from its predators.

Habitat
The place where a plant or animal usually lives is called its habitat.

The desert is the habitat of this bird.

Larva
A young animal which looks quite different from what it will look like when it is fully grown.

Predator
An animal that kills and eats other animals.

Crocodiles are predators. They eat fish, water birds and land animals.

Prey
An animal that is caught and eaten by another animal.

Tide
The rise and fall of the sea level. In most places on the coast this happens twice every day. It happens because the water is pulled by the Moon's gravity.